Cars! Cars! Cars!

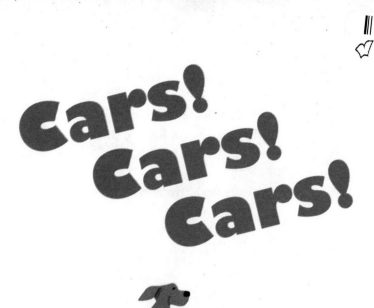

by Grace Maccarone
Illustrated by David A. Carter

SCHOLASTIC INC.

New York Toronto London Auckland Sydney
Mexico City New Delhi Hong Kong

To my cousin Carl,
who has always loved cars.
—G.M.

To Molly and Emma with love.
—D.A.C.

ISBN 0-439-18017-1

Text copyright © 1995 by Grace Maccarone. Illustrations copyright © by David Carter. All rights reserved. Published by Scholastic Inc. SCHOLASTIC and associated logos are trademarks and/or registered trademarks of Scholastic Inc.

12 11 10 9 8 7 6 5 4   0 1 2 3 4 5/0   E

Printed in the U.S.A.   08 MAC

First Scholastic paperback printing, February 2000

One car

Two cars

Old car

New car

Yellow car

Blue car

Many cars

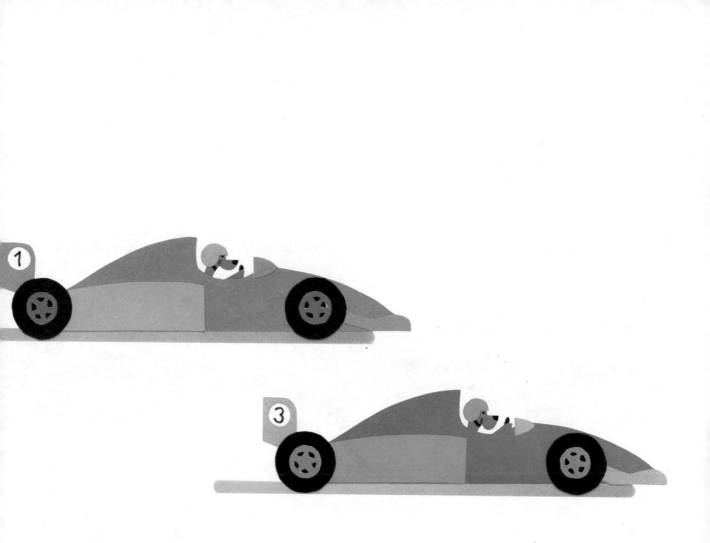

Few cars

Long car

Short car

Limo and

Sports car

Funny car

Odd car

Hot car

Squad car

Long-ago car

Just-for-show car

Fast car

Slow car

"Stop, car!"

"Go, car!"

Low and

High car

Wet car

Dry car

His car

My car

Say good-bye, car!